The NATURAL WORLD of the TURKS AND CAICOS ISLANDS

Written and illustrated by
Katherine Orr

Photographs by
Diane Taylor

DEDICATION

To all the now and future children of these islands

Paperback ISBN: 978-1-7354042-3-3
Ebook ISBN: 978-1-7354042-8-8
© 2021 by Katherine Orr

Printed in the United States of America

Published by NATUREBOOKS
44-119 Bayview Haven Place
Kaneohe, HI, 96744 USA
For all queries and permissions contact
Katherine Orr at www.katherineshelleyorr.com

TABLE OF CONTENTS

Lessons from the past..4
Our islands are a very special place...6
What are our islands made of?..8
How were our islands formed?...10
Red mangroves help build the land...12
How did plants and animals get here?..14
What kind of plants live here?..16
Turks and Caicos heather...18
The Caicos pine tree...19
How are plants important to us?..21
Who are our animal neighbors?...24
The Turks and Caicos rock iguana..28
The air..31
The web of life...32
The seashore..40
Rocky shores..42
Sandy shores 44
Mangrove shores 46
How are mangrove shores important?...48
The sea...50
Coral reefs; How are coral reefs important?...51
Coral reefs can be damaged easily..53
The spiny lobster...54
Seagrass meadows...56
How are seagrass meadows important?...57
The queen conch..58
The turtle...60
The whale..61
Caring for our natural world...62

Lessons from the past

The first people to live in the Turks and Caicos Islands were the Lucayans, who arrived here 1,300 years ago. At that time Grand Turk was covered in trees. Sea turtles nested on the beaches, crocodiles lived along the creeks, giant iguanas and tortoises roamed the land, and red-footed boobies nested along the shore. The Lucayans did not understand how easy it is to damage the natural world. They took these animals for food at a faster pace than nature could replace them. Four hundred years later, all these animals were gone from the Islands, forever.

red-footed boobies

   The Spanish came next. They captured the Lucayans and took them as slaves to Hispaniola. (This is a reminder of what can happen when we do not treat other people with respect, especially those who are different from us.)

   Today we understand that our actions have consequences. Something as simple as shading lights near a beach at night can help baby turtles race to the sea instead of getting confused and going the wrong way.

   Learning from people's experiences in the past can help guide our choices for the future. If we work together and make good choices, we can preserve our lovely natural world for generations to come.

Our islands are a very special place!

   We live in a part of the world
where the climate is warm the year round,
where the seas around us are warm and clear,
where the beaches and the waves are gentle,
where the air is clean and the rain is pure enough for us to drink.
Few places have such a pleasing environment.

In many places harsh climates make life difficult. Some parts of the world are freezing cold with icy oceans and great crashing waves along the shores. Some places have dirtied the air so much that it is unhealthy to breathe and the rainwater is full of poisons. We have not spoiled our natural world. Let's look closely and see what a special place we really have.

What are our islands made of?

The Turks and Caicos Islands are made of limestone. Limestone is a soft, whitish rock. The white color comes from "calcium carbonate". Calcium carbonate, which we sometimes call "lime", is the same white substance that seashells, corals, chalk, and even cement is made of. In some rocks the white may be streaked with pink or brown. Limestone rock along the shore is grey and pitted from the wind and sea. But if you break off a piece you can see it is white inside.

   Because limestone dissolves in water, places where the earth is made of limestone often have underground caves. Our Conch Bar Caves in Middle Caicos are very impressive. They were formed slowly over thousands and thousands of years by water passing through the limestone. As the limestone dissolved and was carried away by water, great spaces were hollowed out underground. There are several smaller caves in our islands. Perhaps some are not yet discovered!

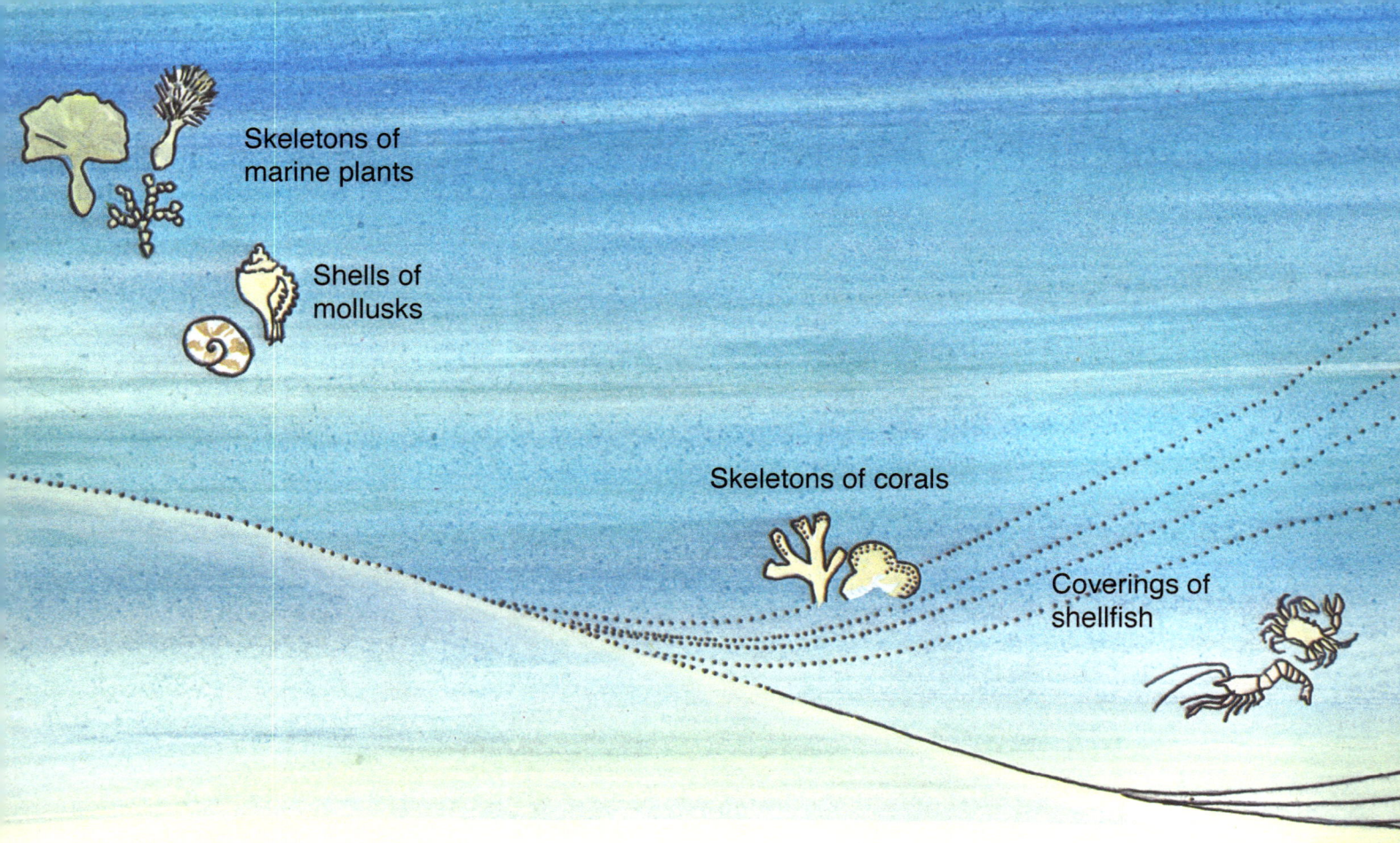

How were our islands formed?

To learn how our limestone islands formed we must start with the story of our sand. The warm seawater around us contains much dissolved calcium carbonate. Animals that live in the sea use this to build their shells and skeletons. Certain plants in the sea build skeletons, too. After these animals and plants die and decay, only their hard shells and skeletons remain. Over time these break down into grains of sand.

There is so much calcium carbonate in our seawater that some of it forms deposits around very tiny particles that drift in the ocean and rest on the sea floor. As these tiny particles become coated with lime they form egg-shaped sand grains called *ooliths*.

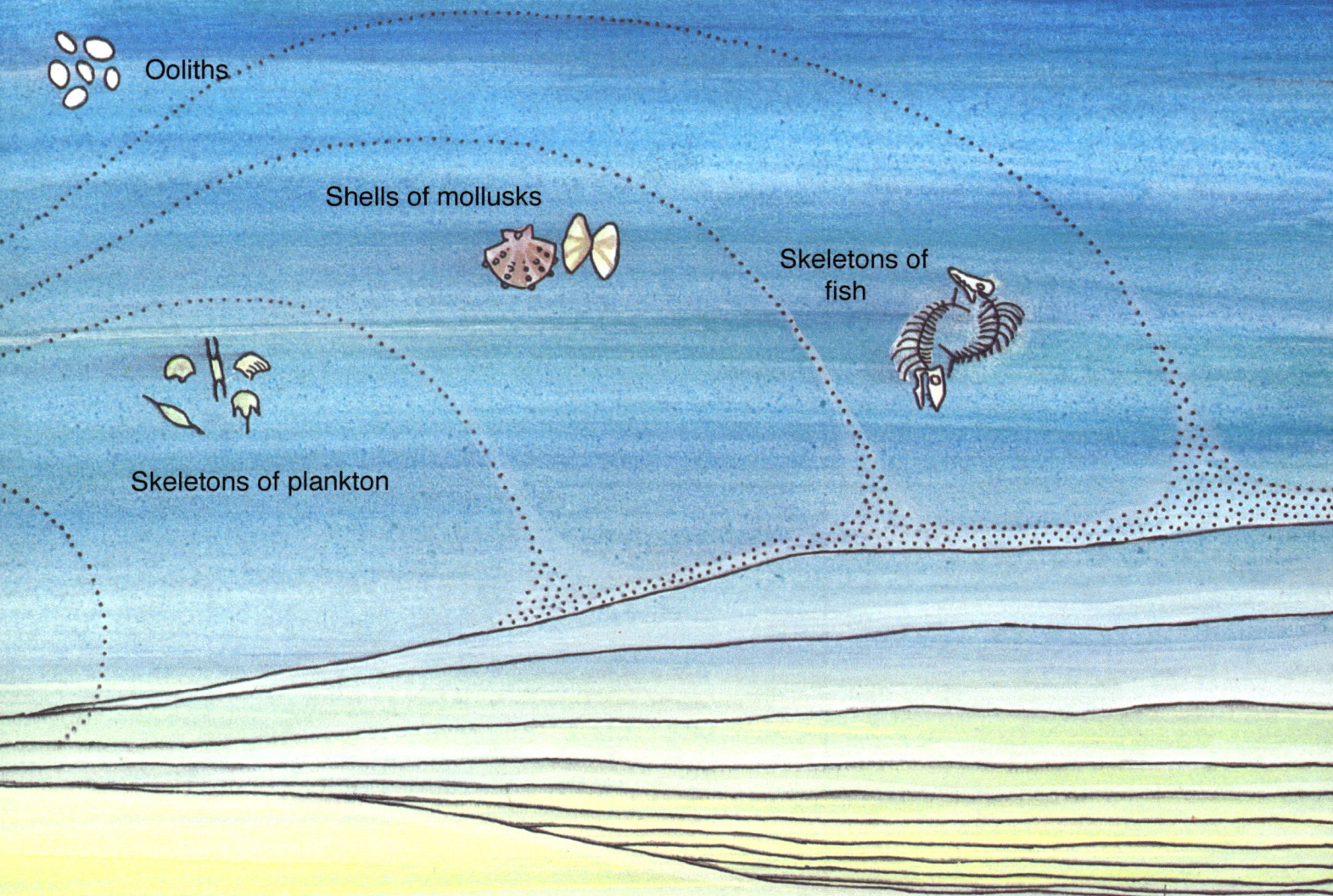

For many millions of years the crumbled shells and skeletons of dead plants and animals, as well as countless tons of ooliths, created white sands. Together these sands collected on the sea bottom, layer upon layer, becoming thicker and heavier over time. The weight of the upper layers pressed on the layers beneath. Gradually the deep layers were pressed together so tightly that they turned into limestone rock.

Over millions of years, the sea level has risen and fallen, exposing the rock and then covering it again with new layers of sand and seawater. Over long spans of time ocean currents carved deep channels in the rock, helping to shape the islands we know today.

Red mangroves help build the land

Strong water currents can carry heavy loads of sand; weak water currents can carry only light loads. As waves and currents strengthen they pick up new sand, and as they weaken they drop it again. In this way, waves and water currents carry sand from place to place. They build sand shoals in one area and wash them away in another. In areas where water currents are gentle and sand shoals are building, red mangroves can help stabilize the sand and build new land. Here's how it works.

Red mangrove trees can live in shallow seawater. Their yellow flowers grow into young plants while still on the parent tree. When the "seedlings" (there is no actual seed) drop from the tree, some take root nearby, while others drift many miles before arriving on distant shores and taking root.

Red mangroves have arching "prop-roots" that grip the sand like the spread fingers of a hand. These special roots help anchor the growing seedlings and they also help hold the sand in place. Many prop roots slow the water currents, causing sand in the water to settle out among the roots. In the same way, mangrove branches slow the wind so it drops wind-blown soil and sand. As new mangrove leaves grow, old leaves die and fall among the roots. Decaying leaves and twigs add nutrients that help build new soil beneath the red mangrove trees.

As this process continues, the ground slowly builds higher and firmer. As the mangroves continue to grow in size and numbers, the new land around them becomes more stable. Storms come, but now the red mangroves help protect the land from being washed away by strong waves.

How did plants and animals get here?

Plants and animals can only reach a new island by sea or by air. The first mangrove trees drifted from another shore as floating seedlings. Seeds such as almonds and coconuts also wash ashore on the beaches and sprout. Giant tree trunks may drift across the sea from far shores carrying insects and lizards. On their journey, these floating logs become homes for crabs, barnacles, and other small marine animals. These sea creatures are then carried to the new shore.

Tiny seeds and insects are blown by the winds to new land. Birds visit the island carrying seeds and insects on their feet and feathers. People who visit the island in boats may bring many new plants and animals with them.

What kinds of plants live here?

All plants living in the wild depend on nature to fill their needs. Each kind of plant has its own set of needs for things like sunlight, water, warmth, and nutrients. Some plants can live well in places with low levels of soil and high levels of salt, sun and wind. Other plants need more shade, food and shelter. We find each kind of plant in the particular place, or "habitat", that meets its needs. A plant's natural habitat is the place where it finds what it needs to live.

In the Turks and Caicos Islands there are many different habitats where some plants can thrive and others cannot. Let's walk around our island. What kinds of plants will we see, and where will we find them?

Along the beach above the high tide line we see grasses growing in the sand. On western shores we might find sea oats growing along the dune. Along eastern shores we might find purslane getting splashed by salty spray. These plants thrive in sandy, salty, seashore habitats.

As we walk inland to dry scrublands near the coast, the hot sun shines and salt is in the air. Here we may find sea grapes, acacia, or prickly pear cactus. Each island has its own community of plants that thrive in dry, limey soils. What do you find on your island?

In dry wooded places where the trees grow taller, the trees help create soil and shade where other plants can live. Here we can look for sapodilly and poisonwood. Bees make safe and flavorful honey from the poisonwood flowers, but don't stand under these trees when it's raining!

In low wetland habitats we can often find tall grass and black mangrove trees. Sometimes we find cabbage palms. These plants thrive in marshy areas with black, mucky soil. In front of the black mangrove, growing in the sea, the red mangrove is the only tree that can grow in salt water.

Some plants are much more common than others because they evolved in habitats that are common and widespread. Other plants are not so common. Some are very rare because they have adapted to life in harsh or unusual habitats where not many other plants can survive. Let's look at two rare plants that call the Turks and Caicos Islands home: the Turks and Caicos heather, and the Caicos pine.

Turks & Caicos heather

The Turks and Caicos Heather is our national flower. There are many kinds of heather growing throughout the world, but this particular one is found only in our islands, growing in a few isolated spots, mainly on Big Ambergris and Salt Cays. Its preferred habitat is along the edges of salinas. The plant itself stands only 30 cm tall and, unlike more common heathers, it has no leaves — the stem does the job that leaves normally do: making food sugars from sunlight (photosynthesis). if you are lucky enough to see this heather in bloom, lean close to enjoy its colorful beauty, and see if you can smell the light fragrance of its flowers.

The Caicos pine tree

Trees help create habitats for other plants and animals by offering them shade, food, and shelter. The Caicos pine creates a habitat that is home for birds, lizards, insects and other plants. Together, the physical environment and the organisms that live there are called an "ecosystem". The Caicos pine ecosystem is unique to our Islands.

The Caicos pine is the national tree of the Turks and Caicos Islands. Pine yards (pine forests) are found only in low-lying places where there is a constant source of salt-free water in the ground. Only two islands and one cay in our country have these conditions: North Caicos, Middle Caicos, and Pine Cay.

The Caicos pines have been under attack from an invasive insect called the pine tortoise scale. Between 2000 and 2010, the scale insect caused 95% of adult Caicos pines to sicken and die. Our pine yards came close to being wiped out. In 2008 The Caicos Pine Recovery Project began working to save this unique pine ecosystem. People and organizations working together, in our country and elsewhere, are making a difference. They are helping the pine yards recover.

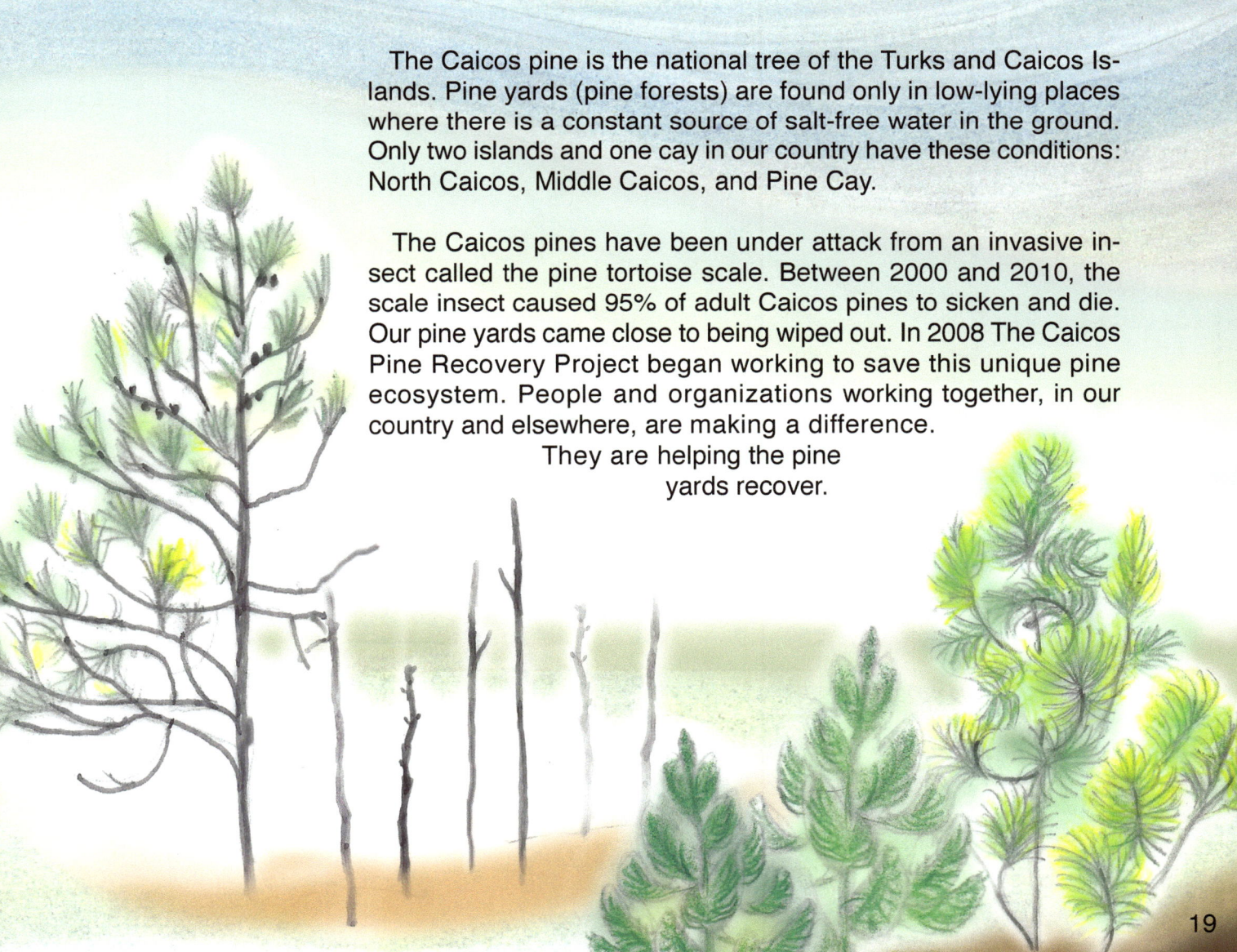

How are plants important to us?

- Trees "catch the rain" so we have water.
- Trees and flowers give us shade and beauty.
- Flowers make the air smell sweet and fresh!
- We can weave many useful things with palm fronds and grasses.
- Plants provide homes and food for our wildlife.
- We can make teas, jellies, and medicines from wild herbs and fruits.

There are more ways that plants are important to us. Can you think of them?

Who are our animal neighbors?

We learned that each kind of plant lives in the particular habitat that meets its life needs. This is true for animals too. Animals live in places where they can find food, shelter, and a safe place to rest, breed and raise their young.

How lucky we are that no dangerous animals live in our islands.

When you go for a walk, how many different kinds of animals can you find? Do you know where to look for them?

Can you identify the animals on these pages and tell where to find them on your island?

Here are some other animals that live in the Turks and Caicos. These animals were brought here by people.

Mice and rats come to our islands on supply boats. When these boats tie up at the dock some mice and rats get off. Mice and rats get into our houses and eat our food. They can spread diseases. In the bush, rats kill baby birds and lizards, including young iguanas.

Mice and rats like garbage.
If we don't spread garbage,
we won't spread mice and rats!

When dogs and cats run wild in the bush they harm our wildlife. Dogs and cats kill birds, lizards and iguanas.

The Turks and Caicos rock iguana

In the past, Turks and Caicos rock iguanas lived throughout most of our islands. Today they exist on only a few islands and small cays. Their numbers have been dwindling for many years, mainly because dogs and cats are killing them in the wild.

Like most other lizards, iguanas lay eggs. In June the female digs a pit in warm sand and lays from 2 to 11 eggs in it. She covers the nest with sand and guards this spot for the first few days or weeks. In about three months time, the eggs hatch and the baby iguanas dig their way to the surface. Now they are on their own. If the youngsters live long enough to reach adulthood in 6-7 years, the males and females will breed and start the cycle of life again.

Iguanas can live twenty years, and more. Males can grow to be 1.6 kg and 80 cm; females are smaller and lighter, with shorter spines along the back.

Our efforts to protect our special neighbor—
this unique rock iguana—are succeeding.
Let's keep up the good work!

Rock iguanas eat mostly leaves, flowers and fruits from a wide variety of plants. Their fondness for fruits makes them one of nature's farmers. Iguanas don't digest the seeds of the fruits they eat. So as they wander around their habitat they spread seeds passed out in their dung. Like farmers, they scatter seeds and fertilizer. This helps their habitat stay healthy.

Remember the giant tortoise that once roamed our islands? We don't want the Turks and Caicos rock iguana to vanish like the tortoise. Today this unique iguana is our largest native land animal. It faces many dangers and has a difficult road ahead, but there is good news. Thanks to the combined efforts of many people all working together, the number of iguanas is no longer falling. It has stabilized, and on some cays the number of iguanas has increased.

The air

The sun and wind are our free gifts.
How many ways can we use them?

- ♦ To dry fruits
  - ♦ To heat water
    - ♦ To make electricity
      - ♦ To pump water
        - ♦ To fly a kite

♦ ♦ Perhaps our greatest gifts are clean air to breathe and clean rainwater to drink.

The web of life

Our creatures of the air are insects and birds. In the next 6 pages birds, bees and butterflies will show us a most important lesson about our natural world. See if you can guess it first.

Butterflies feed on flower nectar... like this sulphur butterfly.

Birds eat seeds from flowering plants ... like these ground doves.

Bees carry pollen from flower to flower, fertilizing the blossoms so they will make seeds and more flowers will grow.

Flowering plants give food and shelter to many insects ... like this grasshopper.

Insects are food for many birds ... like this yellow warbler, or "yellowbird".

So,

   The yellowbird depends upon the insect for food.

   The insect depends upon the plants for food.

   The plants need bees and butterflies
     to fertilize their blossoms
       so they can make seeds
         which ground doves depend on.

This osprey, or fish hawk, feeds on fish it catches from the sea. What do the fish feed on?

All living things depend on each other to stay alive. This is true for us too. If we care about our own future we must take care of our plants, our animals, and our environment. We need them because our future and theirs is the same.

Have you guessed our important lesson? It is this:

Our natural world is composed of living things that all rely on one another in many different ways. Every plant and animal has a special role to play that benefits the whole. Each eats certain kinds of food, and is also a source of food for others. Some animals create homes for others to live in. Many animals share close relationships, each providing something the other needs.

We are all connected to one another in so many important ways that we call this relationship *the web of life*.

The seashore

The seashore, where land meets sea, is the changing edge of our islands. What can rocky shores, sandy shores and mangrove shores tell us about the nature of our islands?

Rocky shores

We have learned that our islands are made out of limestone rock. When we see rocky shorelines we know that here the land is exposed to ocean waves and currents that are strong enough to carry off sand and wear away the rock itself.

Sandy shores

We have learned that ocean waves and currents are always moving sand from place to place. Sandy beaches grow bigger and smaller. Even when the size of a beach doesn't seem to change, the sands are always shifting.

Mangrove shores

We have learned that red mangroves take root in calm waters and help to build and stablilze new land. When we see red mangrove shorelines we know that here the land and waters are more sheltered and protected than along sandy or rocky shores.

Rocky shores

If we visit a rocky shore what animal will we find first? The most common animal is the snail. His hard shell protects him from drying sun and pounding waves. He also has a strong foot to grip the rock so the waves don't knock him off. Snails glide over the rocks eating very tiny plants. What animals eat snails?

Beaded periwinkles can breathe moist air. They live high along the shore where salt spray splashes them but never covers them.

The Sally Lightfoot crab runs in and out of the waves. Her body is flat so she can hug close to the rocks and hide in cracks.

We can find tooth shells along most rocky shores. Turn this snail over and see its "toothy grin".

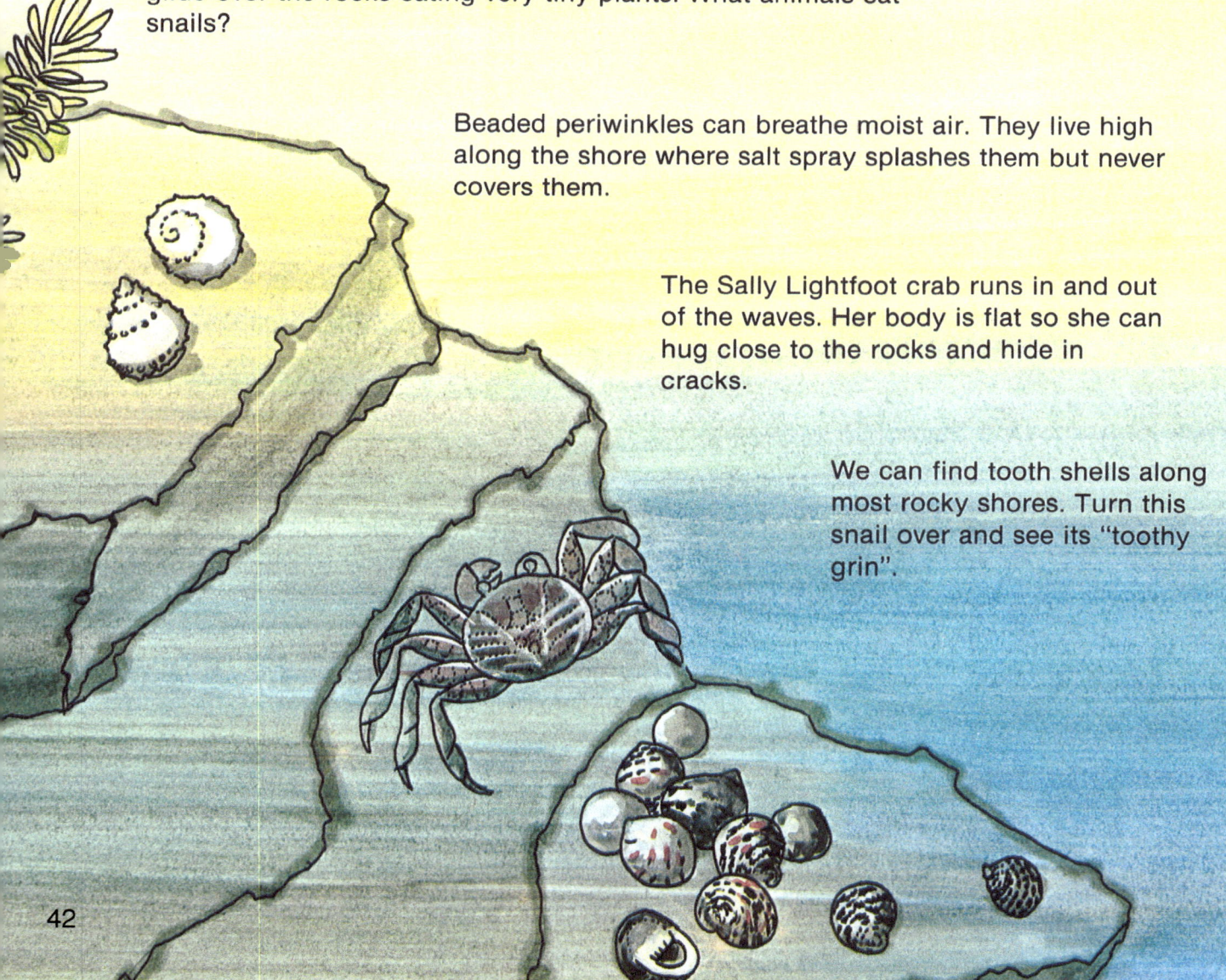

If we wade among the rocks in shallow water what will we find? Underwater rocks make sheltered homes for small fish, sea anemones, tubeworms, and many other sea animals.

We might even find a small octopus. The octopus is not dangerous. It feeds mostly on small shellfish. These animals are very shy and also very intelligent.

Sandy shores

Few animals live on a sandy beach. Here there is little shelter from sun and dryness. Food is scarce.

The animal we see most often on the beach is the ghost crab. This white crab digs a burrow in the sand. He hides inside during the day. At night he comes out to eat insects and bits of food that have washed in from the sea.

Do you know who eats the ghost crab?

On the sand flats we might see a heron wading in the water. He is looking for small fish to eat for supper. Often we see flocks of small shorebirds with long bills. They poke their bills into the sand to eat tiny shrimps and worms.

More animals live in sand that is always underwater. We can find their empty shells washed up on the beach. Can you find some clam shells? A sand dollar?

Mangrove shores

The best way to visit the mangrove shore is by taking a small boat up one of the mangrove creeks. This might be South Creek in Grand Turk, or one of the creeks behind Middle or North Caicos.

The first thing we notice is that the water is warm and very green. The color comes from decaying leaves and very tiny floating plants that turn the water green. Decaying leaves and tiny plants make the creek water into a kind of soup full of food for young animals that live in the sea. The sun heats the water, and the mangroves help protect the area from strong wind and waves.

This is a nice place for baby sea animals to grow. When the babies grow older they will move out of the mangroves to live on the grass beds and reefs.

Among the mangrove's prop-roots we can see schools of baby fish, such as grey snappers, grunts, and even young barracudas.

The prop-roots are covered with seaweeds. Some seaweeds look like tiny green plumes. Other seaweeds look like tiny wine glasses. Small shrimps, crabs, and baby lobsters hide among the seaweeds.

How are mangrove shores important?

◆ Their dense networks of branches and prop-roots create sheltered habitats above and below water, where many living things can thrive.

◆ They are important nursery areas for baby fish, young lobsters, and many other marine animals.

◆ The roots and branches of mangroves help protect land from storm waves and strong winds. The best place to put a boat during a hurricane is in the mangroves.

◆ They are places where many fish and turtles come to feed.

◆ They are places where many birds nest. Some birds that nest in the mangroves are pelicans, night herons, and frigate birds.

The sea

Under the shallow seas of the Turks and Caicos Island banks is a different world. We know the seas around us are important to our daily lives because they give us salt, fish, conch, and lobster to eat. We also get a cool place to bathe when the weather is hot. But there is much more to this undersea world than the seafood and salt we eat.

Earlier in the book, as we walked across our island and visited the Caicos pine yard, we saw that different habitats provide food and shelter for many different kinds of plants and animals. We learned that habitats together with the plants and animals that live there are called "ecosystems". The same holds true beneath the sea. Two important marine ecosystems are coral reefs and seagrass meadows.

Coral reefs

It can be surprising to learn that the stony structures we call coral reefs have been built mostly by tiny coral animals called polyps, each smaller than a pea. Most of the rock that forms a coral reef is dead skeleton left by many generations of living polyps over many thousands of years. Polyps live only on the surface of the corals, like a living skin.

How are coral reefs important?

- Coral reefs support a huge amount and variety of ocean life.
- They protect islands and harbors from destruction by strong waves.
- They provide sources of income from fisheries and tourism.
- They are famous the world over for their unusual beauty.

Let's put on a face mask and go take a look!

Corals grow very slowly. They do not grow fast like plants. Large numbers and varieties of plants and animals live on and around the corals. All of them, together, form the coral reef ecosystem. If a coral reef is damaged or destroyed it will take a very long time to grow back. And it may never grow back without our help. The best way to protect coral reefs is to do them no harm. The list of points on the next page can help us avoid harming coral reefs.

Coral reefs can be damaged easily. Here's what we can do:

◆ Set out moorings so boat anchors don't drag across corals and break them.

◆ Don't collect corals to sell to tourists, or squirt bleach into the coral reef to catch lobsters. Bleach is a poison that kills corals and other reef life that cannot flee from it.

◆ Sometimes people do things along the shoreline that make the water so muddy that corals die. Coral reefs need to live in clean, clear water. We can avoid dirtying our waters so our seas remain clear and our reefs remain alive.

◆ Around the world, temperatures are getting warmer because of human activities. This "global warming" is causing ocean temperatures to rise, which in turn is causing corals to sicken and die. There are solutions to this global problem. We can help by learning about them and then putting them into practice.

Whenever we learn that something we do is causing harm we must be willing to change our ways. Let's take good care of our coral reefs!

The spiny lobster

The spiny lobster is a special reef animal. It is one of our main fisheries export products. But we must be careful. Every year there are fewer lobsters on our reefs because we are taking them from the sea faster than they can replace themselves. Lobsters replace themselves by having lots of babies. If we want to harvest lobsters for many years to come, we must leave enough lobsters in the sea each year to grow the next generation. We need to allow lobsters to reproduce before we harvest them. Our fisheries laws are designed to help us do this.

Four kinds of lobsters in our waters grow big enough to be fished for food. We can identify them by looking at the spots on their tails. The *smooth-tailed* lobster has spots only on the sides of the tail. The *spiny* lobster has two bigger spots on the second tail segment, and the *spotted* lobster's tail has many smaller spots all over it. We know the slipper lobster by its odd body shape.

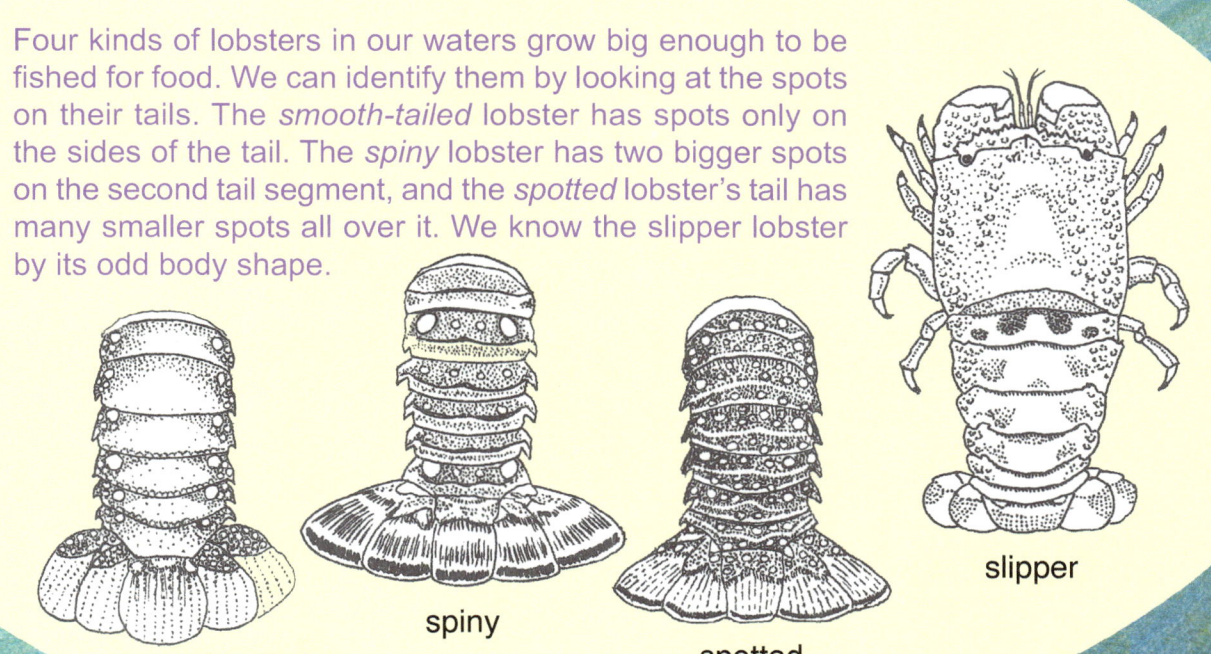

smooth-tailed spiny spotted slipper

Our fisheries laws encourage us to take lobsters whose backs are 9 centimeters (3.5 inches) long or longer. Spiny lobsters smaller than this size are still children. They are not old enough to mate. When we eat shrimp-size lobsters and sell them as packaged lobster meat we are selling and eating our lobster children. Instead, let's protect the places where these children live and help them grow up. By leaving young lobsters in the sea until they have mated and laid eggs at least once, we are helping to protect our fisheries and also the web of life.

Seagrass meadows

Several kinds of seagrasses grow in the shallow waters around our islands. Seagrasses are similar to grasses on land—they have flowers and roots that absorb nutrients. Seagrass meadows (also called seagrass flats and seagrass beds) are fun to explore. They are habitats for clams, snails, worms, sponges, urchins, seaweeds, fish, and more. Animals that live in the seagrass habitat are found over the grass (like the cowfish), on it (like the sea star), and buried among its roots (like worms and clams). How many of the plants and animals on these pages have you seen?

Seagrass meadows, like coral reefs, are important to the health of the ocean and our islands.

How are seagrass meadows important?

◆ They help stabilize the sea bottom.

◆ They provide food and shelter for a wide variety of marine life.

◆ They are nurseries for many coral reef animals.

◆ They help keep ocean water clean, which helps coral reefs.

◆ They are places where many fish and turtles come to feed.

◆ They help protect our coastlines from the effects of storm waves.

◆ They take in carbon dioxide (this helps combat global warming) and they also recycle nutrients.

Young queen conchs look different from their parents: their shells have no broad lips. The conch's shell forms a spiral that wraps around the conch's body as it grows. As the conch nears adulthood, the lip of the shell stops growing in a spiral. It begins to flair outward to form a broad lip. From now on the conch's shell will not grow larger, but the lip will continue to grow thicker as the conch ages.

adult queen conch

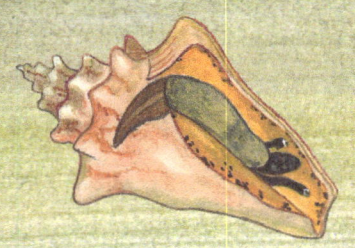

young conchs

The queen conch

The queen conch is an important animal that lives in seagrass meadows around our islands. Like the spiny lobster, it is a valuable food and fisheries product. And like lobsters, conchs are becoming fewer and fewer because we are taking them from the sea faster than they can replace themselves. As we learned from lessons of the past, the only way to keep plants and animals in our future is to allow them to seed the next generations. Enough children must grow up every year to replace the adults we take from the sea.

milk conch

roostertail conch

fighting conch

hawkwing conch

Four smaller conchs share our waters with the queen conch. They are not large or common enough to make a fishery. Nevertheless, each of them contributes in its own special way to the wonderful web of life.

Queen conchs are not ready to mate and lay eggs until they are about three years old. As they near this age the shell begins to form a broad lip. At first the lip is thin, but it thickens over time. A conch shell with a strong, broad lip is a sign that the conch is old enough to reproduce. Until this time, the conch is still growing up. We don't want to eat these growing children; we want to protect them.

59

The turtle

The sea around us holds many mysteries. One of these is the turtle. Although they live in the sea, sea turtles breathe air. They swim great distances across the oceans, and no one knows just where they go and what they do. When a female turtle is ready to lay eggs she returns to the beach where she was born (or hatched) and buries her eggs in the sand.

Because so many turtles and turtle eggs are taken for food, and because the beaches where they nest are so often disturbed, sea turtles around the world are now in danger of disappearing forever. We are very lucky to have turtles still nesting on some of our beaches. We must help these eggs survive and hatch so there will still be turtles in our waters for years to come.

In the waters around our islands we see green, hawksbill, and loggerhead turtles. Can you identify the turtle on this page?

The whale

The humpback whale is another special and mysterious animal of the sea. Whales are the largest animals in the world. And like turtles, they breathe air.

Humpback whales are found throughout the world. Most humpback whales travel long distances across thousands of miles twice every year. They travel between the cold oceans up north where they feed on tiny shrimp-like animals, and the warm oceans of the Caribbean where they breed. During January, February, and March, humpback whales are often seen near our islands. They have come here to give birth and to mate. The Mouchoir Banks and other submerged reefs and banks, including Turks and Caicos, are important "calving" grounds where females give birth (baby whales are called "calves"). As summer approaches, the hungry whales head north again to spend the summer feeding.

Caring for our natural world

We've learned that all plants and animals, including ourselves, are interconnected in a great "web of life". Plants and animals live together in ecosystems, joined by their needs for things like food, water, and safe spaces to live in. A change in one part of the system can throw the whole system off balance. When changes happen slowly, ecosystems can balance and sustain themselves. But today, Earth's environments are changing too quickly, and ecosystems everywhere are under stress. Now, more than ever, it is important for us to focus on caring for our natural world—both our island world, and the world of planet Earth.

The best way to care for nature is to cause it no harm by protecting native wildlife and the environment. When harm has been done, we can take action steps to help reverse the damage. In this book we have learned several things we can do to care for our natural world, including…

- keeping our pet cats and dogs from running wild in the bush and harming wildlife

- avoiding use of chemicals that can poison coral reefs

- learning what our fisheries laws are and why they are important so we feel inspired to follow them.

◆ Also, we can learn to distinguish our local rock iguanas from the invasive green iguanas that are trying to take over. If we see a green iguana we can report it to the TCI Iguana Hotline at tciiguana@gmail.com.

◆ We can pick up rubbish like plastic bottles and bags, and scraps of old fish net as we walk along the shoreline.

◆ We can even help our coral reefs by adopting a small coral growing in an underwater nursery! (Contact Turks and Caicos Reef Fund at tcreef.org)

◆ We can collaborate with other likeminded groups of people around the world. When we all work together for the common good, good things happen!

There are countless ways we can care for our natural world. The ideas in this book are just a start. Learning about nature and helping it to thrive is an exciting adventure. Once you start on this journey the possibilities are endless. But one thing's for sure: many wonderful discoveries and exciting surprises await you along the way!

Acknowledgments

Just as no life form exists in isolation, no book exists in isolation, either. This small nature book, like virtually every other nonfiction endeavor, results from countless influences including the contributions of individuals from all walks of life: explorers, researchers, educators, papermakers and printers, just to name a few. Those who have contributed to our awareness and understanding of nature are too numerous to count, let alone name, but I am grateful to them all for their curiosity, dedication and perseverance—curiosity to explore and discover, the dedication to educate others so the light gets passed on, and the perseverance to continue to protect and defend nature's sacred web of life for the good of all beings.

Special thanks to William F. Keegan, PhD., for his contributions to the first section of this book, **Lessons from the past;** to Marsha Pardee for her many comments and suggestions that have made this a better book; and to my friend, colleague, and collaborator, Dee Taylor, for turning this book journey into a fun shared adventure.

I would also like to acknowledge the memory of my friend, and mentor, Jane Alison Halaby, who helped bring the progenitor of this book to life, forty years ago.

Katherine Orr
(Kathy Hesse)

Katherine (Kathy) Orr sailed into Cockburn Harbour, South Caicos, with her partner, Chuck Hesse, in early 1974. Kathy lived in South Caicos for the next two years, where she studied the ecology and field behavior of the queen conch, *Strombus gigas*. She received her masters degree for this work in 1976 from the University of Connecticut. From 1976 to 1980 she lived on Pine Cay, where she helped develop and teach natural history and biology courses for islanders and visiting students. Following her lifelong passion for exploring the natural world and living in a healthy and sustainable way, Kathy has continued to share her interests and educate others through writing and illustration. She has authored and illustrated numerous books. Visit her website at www.katherineshelleyorr.com

Diane Taylor

Diane (Dee) Taylor is the author of the memoir *The Perfect Galley Book* and *The Gift of Memoir*, and has published numerous nonfiction stories in *Canadian Yachting, Cruising World*, *The Journal of Palliative Care, Times of the Islands*, and other magazines and newspapers. In the early 1980s Diane lived for three years on Pine Cay in the Turks and Caicos Islands, where her work included growing algae to feed baby conch. Returning to Miami, she taught English as a Second Langauge (ESL) to Haitian refugees, then she moved to Canada where she continued to teach ESL at highschools and colleges. She gives a course in memoir writing to encourage others to write down their stories.

www.ingramcontent.com/pod-product-compliance
Lightning Source LLC
Chambersburg PA
CBHW041103070526
44583CB00002B/38